TOUCH

TOUCH

Thom Gunn

FABER & FABER

24 Russell Square London

First published in mcmlxvii
by Faber and Faber Limited
24 Russell Square London WC1
Printed in Great Britain by
Latimer Trend & Co Ltd Plymouth

'Misanthropos' was performed on the B.B.C. Third Programme on 8th March 1965. It was produced by Douglas Cleverdon and read by Alan Dobie and Julian Glover. It was first printed in *Encounter*. 'No Speech from the Scaffold', 'Taylor Street', 'Snowfall', and 'In the Tank' first appeared in *Poetry*, and other poems were first printed in the *Observer*, *Agenda*, *New Statesman*, *Critical Quarterly*, and *Fifteen Poems for William Shakespeare*. Grateful acknowledgments are made to producer and editors.

Contents

The Goddess

When eyeless fish meet her on
her way upward, they gently
turn together in the dark
brooks. But naked and searching
as a wind, she will allow
no hindrance, none, and bursts up

through potholes and narrow flues
seeking an outlet. Unslowed
by fire, rock, water or clay,
she after a time reaches
the soft abundant soil, which
still does not dissipate her

force—for look! sinewy thyme
reeking in the sunlight; rats
breeding, breeding, in their nests;
and the soldier by a park
bench with his greatcoat collar
up, waiting all evening for

a woman, any woman
her dress tight across her ass
as bark in moonlight. Goddess,
Proserpina: it is we,
vulnerable, quivering,
who stay you to abundance.

The Kiss at Bayreuth

Colours drain, shapes blur, resisting,
details swim together, the mass
of the external wobbles, sways,
disintegrating, yet seems to
hesitate before it is sucked
into the eye of the cyclone.

What is this pillar with the eye
that bares and discolours the world,
surrounded by the wash of time?
The inhuman eye contemplates
its own calm inclusive fulness,
its tendency, even, toward death.

The two, their turbulence the kiss
and yet annulled by it, may then
be said to both move and be still,
move in awareness and be still,
to, for one moment and only
that moment, not think of themselves.

Berlin in Ruins

Anhalter Bahnhof

It has an edge, or many edges.
The memory that most recurs is
of bronze Imperial fantasies

squirming with plump hauteur on the one
wall of a brown-brick railway station
soon to be reduced. That great ruin

totters beneath associations.
But you encounter a resistance,
and yourself resist. It is at once

unyielding in texture and fertile.
The mind does not rest without peril
among the tarnished blades of laurel:

it may cut on them, it may fester
—until it throbs with a revived fear
of the dark hysteric conqueror

returning from France in triumph as
the hectic that overtakes process,
beneath a silk tent of swastikas.

And fever may descend on the brow
like the high circlet, in whose shadow
the mind awakes, bathed in poison now;

or, harder and sharper than bronze, still
supporting the insupportable,
it may survive its own stiff laurel.

Bravery

on a painting by Chuck Arnett

What a romantic picture!
his back is toward us, yet
he is practically
a silhouette, black, he
is brave with separation—

and he is set against
an indeterminate pale
grey-and-yellow country, he is
about to step on
or into the smoky
swirl of a fog-
trough or river.

I visualize his
first step: as his heroic
foot presses down
on the spongy district,
a curl of mist that lapped
the heel curdles, a
glint of spray on
the toe dulls
to mud, and the first step will
suck the country dry.

For he has become his
outline, and holds no
warm clutter of detail.

Giant vampire! if your
back were not turned, I
should have known you
before, you are
my monstrous lover, whom
I gaze at
every time I shave.

Confessions of the Life Artist

I

'Whatever is here, it is
material for my art.

On the extreme shore of land,
and facing the disordered
rhythms of the sea, I taste
a summoning on the air.

I derive from these rocks, which
inhibit the sea's impulse.
But it is a condition,
once accepted, like air: air
haunted by the taste of salt.

II

I think, therefore I cannot
avoid thought of the morrow.
Outside the window, the birds
of the air and the lily
have lost themselves in action.
I think of the birds that sleep
in flight, of the lily's pale
waxy gleaming, of myself,
and of the morrow pending.
The one thing clear is that I
must not lose myself in thought.

III

You control what you can, and
use what you cannot.
                        Heady,
to hover above the winds,
buoyant with a sense of choice.
Circling over a city,
to reject the thousand, and
to select the one. To watch
the goodly people there, to
know that their blood circulates,
that it races as yours does,
live between extremities.

IV

But what of the unchosen?

They are as if dead. Their deaths,
now, validate the chosen.

Of course, being left as dead
may lead to the thing itself.
I read about them: and what
could be more fortifying
to one's own identity
than another's suicide?

If there are forbidden arts,
mine must indeed be of them.

V

She is immersed in despair,
but I am here, luckily.
She, become indefinite,
leans on me who am starkly
redefined at each moment,
aware of her need, and trained
to have few needs of my own.

As I support her, so, with
my magnificent control,
I suddenly ask: 'What if
she has the edge over me?'

VI

To give way to all passions,
I know, is merely whoring.
Yes, but to give way to none
is to be a whore-master.

I stride through the whore-house
when my girls are off duty,
I load them with chocolates,
but cannot for one moment
possess red hair like hers, fresh
cheeks or bee-stung lips like hers,
or a wasteful heart like hers.

VII

I elevate not what I
have, but what I wish to have,
and see myself in others.

There is a girl in the train
who emulates the bee-hive
of the magazine stars of
four years ago.
                    I blush at
the jibes that grow inside me,
lest someone should utter them.

Why was something evolved so
tender, so open to pain?

VIII

Here is a famous picture.

It is of a little Jew
in Warsaw, some years ago,
being hustled somewhere. His
mother dressed him that morning
warmly in cap and cloth coat.
He stares at the camera
as he passes. Whatever
those big shining dark eyes have
just looked on, they can see now
no appeal in the wide world.

IX

I grow old in the design.

Prophecies become fulfilled,
though never as expected,
almost accidentally,
in fact, as if to conform
to some alien order.

But I am concerned with my
own knowledge that the design
is everywhere ethical
and harmonious: circles
start to close, lines to balance.

X

The art of designing life
is no excuse for that life.

People will forget Shakespeare.
He will lie with George Formby
and me, here where the swine root.
Later, the solar system
will flare up and fall into
space, irretrievably lost.

For the loss, as for the life,
there will be no excuse, there
is no justification.'

No Speech from the Scaffold

There will be no speech from
the scaffold, the scene must
be its own commentary.

The glossy chipped
surface of the block is like
something for kitchen use.

And the masked man with his
chopper: we know him: he
works in a warehouse nearby.

Last, the prisoner, he
is pale, he walks through
the dewy grass, nodding

a goodbye to acquaintances.
There will be no speech. And we
have forgotten his offence.

What he did is, now,
immaterial. It is the
execution that matters, or,

rather, it is his conduct
as he rests there, while
he is still a human.

Breakfast

For two years I looked forward
only to breakfast. The night
was not night, it was tempered
by hotel signs opposite.

Yet I must have dozed, for all
at once I would distinguish
loaf and cup, monumental
on the sill's ginger varnish.

I do not mean that breakfast
was a remedy—still less
a ritual—but that toast
and coffee served as markers.

Unsour pungency, hot and
dark, sank down my throat. Dry rough
substance encountered the grind
of my teeth. These were enough,

were properties, as it were,
for a tenacity. I
would now get up from the chair,
to look for a job, or try

phoning my ex-wife. Without
future I had to keep on
—without love, without hope, but
without renunciation.

Taylor Street

The small porch of imitation
marble is never sunny, but
outside the front door he
sits on his kitchen chair facing
the street. In the bent yellowish
face, from under the brim
of a floppy brown hat,
his small eyes watch what
he is not living. But he
lives what he can:
watches without a smile, with
a certain strain, the warmth
of his big crumpled
body anxiously cupped
by himself in himself, as
he leans over himself not
over the cold railing, unmoving but carefully getting
a little strength from the sight of the
passers-by. He has it
all planned: he will live
here morning by morning.

Touch

You are already
asleep. I lower
myself in next to
you, my skin slightly
numb with the restraint
of habits, the patina of
self, the black frost
of outsideness, so that even
unclothed it is
a resilient chilly
hardness, a superficially
malleable, dead
rubbery texture.

You are a mound
of bedclothes, where the cat
in sleep braces
its paws against your
calf through the blankets,
and kneads each paw in turn.

Meanwhile and slowly
I feel a is it
my own warmth surfacing or
the ferment of your whole
body that in darkness beneath
the cover is stealing
bit by bit to break
down that chill.

You turn and
hold me tightly, do
you know who
I am or am I
your mother or
the nearest human being to
hold on to in a
dreamed pogrom.

What I, now loosened,
sink into is an old
big place, it is
there already, for
you are already
there, and the cat
got there before you, yet
it is hard to locate.
What is more, the place is
not found but seeps
from our touch in
continuous creation, dark
enclosing cocoon round
ourselves alone, dark
wide realm where we
walk with everyone.

The Vigil of Corpus Christi

Swaddled to his nose against the chill
he stood all night, like a sentinel
at limits, by the pitted stone wall.

His body was scattered; each grease clot,
each lump and fold in the stiff blanket,
the aches, the circle of his wide hat

touched him at unrelated edges.
But perched above the blanket, his eyes
persisted, trying to become as

steadfast as the dark confronting them.
Then the sky paled: night relinquished him,
like seas casting him up whole through foam.

A footbath clattered in the distance;
his dog ran up and licked him. Each sense
tested itself, sharp from abeyance.

Was this, then, the end of any quest?
the invasion of himself at last
merely by himself? 'To be steadfast,'

he breathed: like a soldier, he straightened.
But the moist tongue went on working round
his ankles; and then, slowly, he grinned

with an unsoldierly joy, at this
soft sweet power awake in his own mass
balanced on his two feet, this fulness.

Misanthropos

to Tony Tanner and Don Doody

The Last Man   *I*

He avoids the momentous rhythm
of the sea, one hill suffices him
who has the entire world to choose from.

He melts through the brown and green silence
inspecting his traps, is lost in dense
thicket, or appears among great stones.

He builds no watch tower. He lives like
the birds, self-contained they hop and peck;
he could conceal himself for a week;

and he learns like them to keep movement
on the undipped wing of the present.
But sometimes when he wakes, with the print

of stone in his side, a relentless
memory of monstrous battle is
keener than counsel of the senses.

He opens, then, a disused channel
to the onset of hatred, until
the final man walks the final hill

without thought or feeling, as before.
If he preserves himself in nature,
it is as a lived caricature

of the race he happens to survive.
He is clothed in dirt. He lacks motive.
He is wholly representative.

II

At last my shout is answered! Are you near,
Man whom I cannot see but can hear?

                                            Here.

The canyon hides you well, which well defended.
Sir, tell me, is the long war ended?

                                          Ended.

I passed no human on my trip, a slow one.
Is it your luck, down there, to know one?

                                         No one.

What have I left, who stood among mankind,
When the firm base is undermined?

                                        A mind.

Yet, with a vacant landscape as its mirror,
What can it choose, to ease the terror?

                                         Error.

Is there no feeling, then, that I can trust,
In spite of what we have discussed?

                                      Disgust.

III

Earlier, travelling on the roads where grass
Softened the gutters for the marsh-bird's nest,
He walked barefoot already, and already
His uniform was peeling from his back.
And coming to this hill across the plain,
He sloughed it bit by bit. Now that, alone,
He cannot seek himself as messenger,
Or bear dispatches between elm and oak,
It is a clumsy frock he starts to fashion
From skins of mole and rabbit; he considers
That one who wears it is without a role.
But the curled darling who survives the war
Has merely lost the admirers of those curls
That always lavished most warmth on his neck;
Though no one sees him, though it is the wind
Utters ambiguous orders from the plain,
Though nodding foxgloves are his only girls,
His poverty is a sort of uniform.
With a bone needle he pursues himself,
Stitching the patchwork spread across his lap,
A courier after identity, and sees
A pattern grow among the disarray.

IV

The moon appears, distinct where all is dim,
And steady in the orbit it must go.
He lies in shadow, then light reaches him.
While, there! the Milky Way follows below,
A luminous field that swings across the sky.
The ancient rhythm almost comforts, slow
Bright mild recurrence that he might move by,
Obedient in the act of breath, and lit,
Mere life, by matter travelling sure and high.
But this is envy for the inanimate,
The youth of things. On the dead globe he sees
Markings as one might on the earth from it,
Where relics of emergent matter freeze.
Down here, two more births followed on the first:
Life, consciousness, like linked catastrophes.
Their sequence in him cannot be reversed
Except in death, thus, when the features set.
Meanwhile he must live, as he looks, immersed
In consciousness that plots its own end yet;
And since the plotter through success would lose
Knowledge of it, he must without regret
Accept the inheritance he did not choose,
As he accepted drafting for that war
That was not of his choosing. He must use
The heaviness, the flaw, he always bore.
The imperfect moon swims forward on its course;
Yet, bathed by shade now, he imagines more—
The clearest light in the whole universe.

V

Green overtaking green, it's
endless: squat grasses creep up,
briars cross, heavily weighed
branches overhang, thickets
crowd in on the brown earth gap
in green which is the path made

by his repeated tread, which,
enacting the wish to move,
is defined by avoidance
of loose ground, of rock and ditch,
of thorn-brimmed hollows, and of
poisoned beds. The ground hardens.

Bare within limits. The trick
is to stay free within them.
The path branches, branches still,
returning to itself, like
a discovering system,
or process made visible.

It rains. He climbs up the hill.
Drops are isolate on leaves,
big and clear. It is cool, and
he breathes the barbarous smell
of the wet earth. Nothing moves
at the edges of the mind.

Memoirs of the World   VI

It has turned cold. I have been gathering wood,
Numb-fingered, hardly feeling what I touched,
Turning crisp leaves to pick up where I could
The damp sticks from beneath them. I have crouched
Piling them up to dry, all afternoon,
And have heard all afternoon, over and over,
Two falling notes—a sweet disconsolate tune,
As if the bird called, from its twiggy cover,
Nót now, nót now, nót now.

I dislodge sticks for kindling, one by one,
From brambles. Struck by shade, I stand and see
Half-blinding me, the cold red setting sun
Through the meshed branches of a leafless tree.
It calls old sunsets to my mind, one most
Which coloured, similarly, the white grey, blackened
Iron and slabbed concrete of a sentry post
With its cold orange. Let me live, one second,
Nót now, nót now, nót now.

Most poignant and most weakening, that recall.
Although I lived from day to day, too, there.
Yet the comparison makes me sensible
Of the diminishing warmth and light, which were,
Or seem to have been, diminished less than now.
The bird stops. Hardening in the single present,
I know, hearing wind rattle in a bough,
I have always harked thus after an incessant
Nót now, nót now, nót now.

VII

Who was it in dark glasses?
Nobody in the street could
see if my eyes were open.
I took them off for movies
and sleep. I waited, I stood
an armed angel among men.

Between the dart of colours
I wore a darkening and
perceived an exact structure,
a chart of the world. The coarse
menace of line was deepened,
and light was slightly impure.

Yet as I lingered there was,
I noticed, continual
and faint, an indecision,
a hunger in the senses.
I would devour the thin wail
of foghorns, or abandon

my whole self time after time
to the chipped glossy surface
of some doorjamb, for instance,
cramming my nail with its grime,
stroking humps where colourless
paint had filled faults to substance.

I was presence without full
being; but from the corner,
in the mere fact of movement,
was I entering the role
of spy or spied on, master
or the world's abject servant?

35

VIII

Dryads, reposing in the bark's hard silence,
Circled about the edges of my fire,
Exact in being, absolute in balance,
Instruct me how to find here my desire:

To separate the matter from its burning,
Where, in the flux that your composures lack,
Each into other constantly is turning.
In the glowing fall of ash—rose, grey, and black,

I search for meaning, studying to remember
What the world was, and meant. Therefore I try
To reconstruct it in a dying ember,
And wonder, does fire make it live or die?

And evil everywhere or nowhere, stealing
Out of my reach, on air, shows like a spark.
I think I grasp it. The momentary feeling
Is merely pain, evil's external mark.

The neighbouring cinders redden now together,
Like earlier worlds to search, where I am shown
Only myself, although I seek another,
A man who burnt from sympathy alone.

IX

A serving man. Curled my hair,
wore gloves in my cap. I served
all degrees and both sexes.
But I gave readily from
the largess of high spirits,
a sturdy body and strong

fingers. Nor was I servile.
No passer-by could resist
the fragrant impulse nodding
upon my smile. I laboured
to become a god of charm,
an untirable giver.

Needing me, needing me, 'Quick!'
they would call: I came gladly.
Even as I served them sweets
I served myself a trencher
of human flesh in some dark
sour pantry, and munched from it.

My diet, now, is berries,
water, and the gristle of
rodents. I brought myself here,
widening the solitude
till it was absolute. But
at times I am ravenous.

X

All that snow pains my eyes, but I stare
on, stare on, lying in my shelter,

feverish, out at the emptiness.
A negative of matter, it is

a dead white surface at random crossed
by thin twigs and bird-tracks on the crust

like fragments of black netting: hard, cold,
wind-swept. But now my mind loses hold

and, servant to an unhinged body,
becoming of it, sinks rapidly

beneath the stitched furs I'm swaddled in,
beneath the stink of my trembling skin,

till it enters the heart of fever,
as its captive, unable to stir.

I watch the cells swimming in concert
like nebulae, calm, without effort,

great clear globes, pink and white.—But look at
the intruder with blurred outline that

glides in among the shoals, colourless,
with tendrils like an anemone's

drifting all around it like long fur,
gently, unintelligently. Where

it touches it holds, in an act of
enfolding, possessing, merging love.

There is coupling where no such should be.
Surely it is a devil, surely

it is life's parody I see, which
enthralls a universe with its rich

heavy passion, leaving behind it
gorgeous mutations only, then night.

It ends. I open my eyes to snow.
I can sleep now; as I drowse I know

I must keep to the world's bare surface,
I must perceive, and perceive what is:

for though the hold of perception must
harden but diminish, like the frost,

yet still there may be something retained
against the inevitable end.

XI

Epitaph for Anton Schmidt

The Schmidts obeyed, and marched on Poland.
And there an Anton Schmidt, Feldwebel,
Performed uncommon things, not safe,
Nor glamorous, nor profitable.

Was the expression on his face
'Reposeful and humane good nature'?
Or did he look like any Schmidt,
Of slow and undisclosing feature?

I know he had unusual eyes,
Whose power no orders might determine,
Not to mistake the men he saw,
As others did, for gods or vermin.

For five months, till his execution,
Aware that action has its dangers,
He helped the Jews to get away
—Another race at that, and strangers.

He never did mistake for bondage
The military job, the chances,
The limits; he did not submit
To the blackmail of his circumstances.

I see him in the Polish snow,
His muddy wrappings small protection,
Breathing the cold air of his freedom
And treading a distinct direction.

Elegy on the Dust   *XII*

The upper slopes are busy with the cricket;
  But downhill, hidden in the thicket,
Birds alternate with sudden piercing calls
  The rustling from small animals
Retreating, venturing, as they hunt and breed
  Interdependent in that shade.

Beneath it, glare and silence cow the brain
  Where, troughed between the hill and plain,
The expanse of dust waits: acres calm and deep,
  Swathes folded on themselves in sleep
Or waves that, as if frozen in mid-roll,
  Hang in ridged rows. They cannot fall,
Yet imperceptibly they shift, at flood,
  In quiet encroachment on the wood—
First touching stalk and leaf with silvery cast,
  They block the pores to death at last
And drift in silky banks around the trunk,
  Where dock and fern are fathoms sunk.

Yet farther from the hill the bowl of dust
  Is open to the casual gust
That dives upon its silence, teasing it
  Into a spasm of wild grit.
Here it lies unprotected from the plain,
  And vexed with constant loss and gain,
It seems, of the world's refuse and debris,
  Turns to a vaguely heaving sea,
Where its own eddies, spouts, and calms appear.
  But seas contain a graveyard: here

The graveyard is the sea, material things
   —From stone to claw, scale, pelt and wings—
Are all reduced to one form and one size.
   And here the human race, too, lies
An imperfection endlessly refined
   By the imperfection of the mind.
They have all come who sought distinction hard
   To this universal knacker's yard,
Blood dried, flesh shrivelled, and bone decimated:
   Motion of life is thus repeated,
A process ultimately without pain
   As they are broken down again.
The remnants of their guilt mix as they must
   And average out in grains of dust
Too light to act, too small to harm, too fine
   To simper or betray or whine.

Each colourless hard grain is now distinct,
   In no way to its neighbour linked,
Yet from wind's unpremeditated labours
   It drifts in concord with its neighbours,
Perfect community in its behaviour.
   It yields to what it sought, a saviour:
Scattered and gathered, irregularly blown,
   Now sheltered by a ridge or stone,
Now lifted on strong upper winds, and hurled
   In endless hurry round the world.

The First Man   XIII

The present is a secure place to inhabit,
The past being fallen from the mind, the future
A repetition, only, with variations:
The same mouse on its haunches, nibbling, absorbed,
Another piece of root between the forefeet
Slender as wishbones; the woodlice, silvery balls;
The leaves still falling in vestiges of light.

Is he a man? If man is cogitation,
This is at most a rudimentary man,
An unreflecting organ of perception;
Slow as a bull, in moving; yet, in taking,
Quick as an adder. He does not dream at night.

Echo is in the past, the snow long past,
The year has recovered and put forth many times.

He is bent, looks smaller, and is furred, it seems.
Mole-like he crouches over mounds of dirt,
Sifting. His eyes have sunk behind huge brows.
His nostrils twitch, distinguishing one by one
The smells of the unseen that blend to make
The black smell of the earth, smell of the Mother,
Smell of her food: pale tender smell of worms,
Tough sweet smell of her roots. He is a nose.
He picks through the turned earth, and eats. A mouth.

If he is man, he is the first man lurking
In a thicket of time. The mesh of green grows tighter.
There is yew, and oak picked out with mistletoe.
Watch, he is darkening in the heavy shade
Of trunks that thicken in the ivy's grip.

XIV

'What is it? What?'
Mouth struggles with the words that mind forgot.
  While from the high brown swell
He watches it, the smudge, he sees it grow
As it crawls closer, crawls unturnable
And unforeseen upon the plain below.

'That must be men.'
Knowledge invades him, yet he shrinks again
  And sickens to live still
Upon the green slopes of his isolation,
The 'final man upon a final hill,'
As if he did a sort of expiation.

And now he dreams
Of a shadowed pool nearby fed by two streams:
  If he washed there, he might,
Skin tautened from the chill, emerge above,
Inhuman as a star, as cold, as white,
Freed from all dust. And yet he does not move.

Could he assert
To men who climb up in their journey's dirt
  That clean was separate?
The dirt would dry back, hardening in the heat:
Perpetual that unease, that world of grit
Breathed in, and gathered on the hands and feet.

He is unaware
Of the change already taking place as there,
    In the cold clear early light
He, lingering on the scorched grass wet with dew,
Still hunched but now a little more upright,
In picturing man almost becomes man too.

XV

Hidden behind a rock, he watches, grown
As stony as a lizard poised on stone.
Below, the indeterminate shape flows steady
From plain to wood, from wood to slope. Already
Sharp outlines break, in movement, from the edge.
Then in approach upon the final ridge
It is slowly lost to sight, but he can hear
The shingle move with feet. Then they appear,
Being forty men and women, twos and threes,
Over the rim. From where he is he sees
One of the last men stumble, separate,
Up to the rock, this rock, and lean on it.
You can hear him gulp for wind, he is so close,
You can hear his hand rasp on the shrivelled moss
Blotching the rock: by peering you can see
What a ribbed bony creature it must be,
Sweat streaking dirt at collar-bones and spine,
Sores round the mouth disfiguring the line.

And on the thin chest two long parallel
Clear curving scratches are discernible.
Recent, for only now the drops within
Steal through the white torn edges of the skin
To mix with dirt. Round here, such cuts are common.
It is not hard to visualize the human,
Tired, walking upward on a wooded slant;
Keeping his eyes upon the ground in front,
He made his way round some dropped rotten limb,
And a hanging briar unnoticed swung at him.
And only later does it start to sting.
That wood has its own way of countering.

The watcher is disturbed, not knowing why.
He has with obstinate equanimity,
Unmoving and unmoved, watched all the rest,
But seeing the trivial scratches on the chest,
He frowns. And he performs an action next
So unconsidered that he is perplexed,
Even in performing it, by what it means—
He walks around to where the creature leans.
The creature sees him, jumps back, staggers, calls,
Then, losing balance on the pebbles, falls.

Now that he has moved toward, through, and beyond
The impulse he does not yet understand,
He must continue where he has begun,
Finding, as when a cloud slips from the sun,
He has entered, without stirring, on a field
The same and yet more green and more detailed,
Each act of growth discovered by his gaze;
Yet if the place is changed by what surveys,
He is surveyed and he himself is changed,
Bombarded by perceptions, rearranged—
Rays on the skin investing with a shape,
A clarity he cannot well escape.

He stops, bewildered by his force, and then
Lifts up the other to his feet again.

XVI

Others approach, and I grip
his arm. For it seems to me
they file past my mind, my mind
perched on this bare rock, watching.

They turn and look at me full,
and as they pass they name me.

What is the name Adam speaks
after the schedule of beasts?

Though I grip his arm, the man,
the scratched man, seems among them,
and as he pauses the old
bitter dizziness hits me:
I almost fall. The stale stench!
the hang-dog eyes, the pursed mouth!
no hero or saint, that one.

It is a bare world, and lacks
history; I am neither
his lord nor his servant.

By an act of memory,
I make the recognition:
I stretch out the word to him
from which conversations start,
naming him, also, by name.

XVII

Others approach. Well, this one may show trust
    Around whose arm his fingers fit.
The touched arm feels of dust, mixing with dust
    On the hand that touches it.

And yet a path is dust, or it is none,
    —Merely unstable mud, or weeds,
Or a stream that quietly slips on and on
    Through the undergrowth it feeds.

His own flesh, which he hardly feels, feels dust
    Raised by the war both partly caused
And partly fought, and yet survived. You must,
    If you can, pause; and, paused,

Turn out toward others, meeting their look at full,
    Until you have completely stared
On all there is to see. Immeasurable,
    The dust yet to be shared.

Snowfall

It is no wonder
People look circumspect against the white:
Sharp-edged, darkly filled-in; the creature's heat
Being closely hoarded under
Layers of wool, long coats, and scarves pulled tight.
The element is dazzling and complete:
The floor they tread is bright.

Unseen below
Stir brooks that, under hard panes withdrawn deep,
Still work a secret network through the land
With iced and darkened flow.
Joining, dividing, through black earth, they creep
And honeycomb the country where I stand
With galleries of their sleep.

And here, the floor
Is founded on them: I can see or guess
It follows subterranean bay and fall,
Like them in each contour.
Yet unlike—what the ice-packed heel must press
Not quite resistant, not quite palpable,
I find an edgelessness.

The Girl of Live Marble

She looks to see, and not to seek.
Yet in the candour of her eyes
And in the quick flesh of her cheek
—Rounding compact at the lips' rise—
The seeker comes to his own rest,
Thinking he finds at last an essence
Through merging surfaces expressed
And her unformulable presence.

She is like a cat upon a wall,
As self-contained, as unaware
How far, on each side, is the fall.
None of her acts he longs to share,
None of her qualities extend
Beyond the adequacy she is.
Nor do her lips in motion spend
Anything but inanities.

Nothing, besides, could compromise
The image he has watched appear
Where the pale iris marks her eyes.
O Otherness, impervious, near!
To own it now! . . . But as the watcher
Moves close, it is himself he sees
On the bright convex—clear in feature,
Little, and caught by darknesses.

In the Tank

A man sat in the felon's tank, alone,
Fearful, ungrateful, in a cell for two.
And from his metal bunk, the lower one,
He studied where he was, as felons do.

The cell was clean and cornered, and contained
A bowl, grey gritty soap, and paper towels,
A mattress lumpy and not over-stained,
Also a toilet, for the felon's bowels.

He could see clearly all there was to see,
And later when the lights flicked off at nine
He saw as clearly all there was to see:
An order without colour, bulk, or line.

And then he knew exactly where he sat.
For though the total riches could not fail
—Red weathered brick, fountains, wisteria—yet
Still they contained the silence of a jail,

The jail contained a tank, the tank contained
A box, a mere suspension, at the centre,
Where there was nothing left to understand,
And where he must re-enter and re-enter.

Pierce Street

Nobody home. Long threads of sunlight slant
Past curtains, blind, and slat, through the warm room.
The beams are dazzling, but, random and scant,
Pierce where they end
                  small areas of the gloom
On curve of chairleg or a green stalk's bend.

I start exploring. Beds and canvases
Are shapes in each room off the corridor,
Their colours muted, square thick presences
Rising between
                  the ceiling and the floor,
A furniture inferred much more than seen.

Here in the seventh room my search is done.
A bluefly circles, irregular and faint.
And round the wall above me friezes run:
Fixed figures drawn
                  in charcoal or in paint.
Out of night now the flesh-tint starts to dawn.

Some stand there as if muffled from the cold,
Some naked in it, the wind around a roof.
But armed, their holsters as if tipped with gold.
And twice life-size—
                  in line, in groups, aloof,
They all stare down with large abstracted eyes.

A silent garrison, and always there,
They are the soldiers of the imagination
Produced by it to guard it everywhere.
Bodied within
                the limits of their station
As, also, I am bodied in my skin,

They vigilantly preserve as they prevent
And are the thing they guard, having some time stood
Where the painter reached to make them permanent.
The floorboards creak.
                        The house smells of its wood.
Those who are transitory can move and speak.

The Produce District

What's there to do on Sundays? Sooner do
this than booze.

After the businesses had moved, before
The wrecking started
For the high-rise blocks:
An interim:
Whoever walked along these streets
Found it was shared with him
Only by pigeons, single or in flocks.

Where each night trucks had waited
By warehouse and worn ramp
With oranges or celery to unload,
Now it was smell of must, rot, fungus, damp.
The crumbling and decay accelerated,
Old mattresses and boards in heaps
Losing their colours with their shapes,
The smaller things
Blending like humus, on the road.
And silence—no, small creaks,
Small patterings,
While now, above, the thump and whirr of wings.
The pigeons, grey on grey,
In greater number
Than ever here before
Pecked round the rotting lumber,
Perched on the roofs and walls,
Or wheeled between the faded signs
And broken ornamental scrolls.

I watched the work of spiders, rats, and rain,
And turning on to Front Street found
I was not there alone.
He stood unmoving on the littered ground
In bright scrubbed denims
An airgun loosely in his hands
Staring at something overhead.

Shooting at birds, he said.
I looked at his short greying hair;
His face, lined, hard and ruddy, any age,
Cracking into a smile;
And stood beside him while
He aimed at a parapet some forty-five yards off.
A bang. One pigeon as the others rose
A lump of fluff
Dropped from among them lightly to the street.

Cool air, high fog, and underfoot
Through soft mould, shapes felt like uneven root
Ridging a forest floor.
The place losing itself, lost now, unnamed,
Birds wheeling back, with a low threshing sound.
He aimed
And then once more
I heard the gun repeat
Its accurate answer to the wilderness,
Echoing it and making it complete.
And maple shoots pushed upward through the ground.

Back to Life

Around the little park
The lamps blink on, and make the dusk seem deeper.
I saunter toward them on the grass
That suddenly rustles from the dew,
Hearing behind, at times,
A fragmentary shout or distant bark.
I am alone, like a patrolling keeper.
And then I catch the smell of limes
Coming and going faintly on the dark:
Bunched black at equal height
They stand between the lamps, yet where
They branch out toward them on each side, a few
Touching the lighted glass,
Their leaves are soft green on the night,
The closest losing even their mass,
Edged but transparent as if they too gave light.

The street is full, the quiet is broken.
I notice that the other strollers there
Extend themselves, at ease
As if just woken
To a world they have not yet recovered, though
They move across the dusk, alert,
And stare,
As I do, into shops or at the trees,
Devouring each detail, from leaf to dirt,
In the measured mildness of the air.
Here by the kerb
The boys and girls walk, jostling as they grow,
Cocky with surplus strength.
And weakening with each move, the old,

Cushioned with papers or with rugs
On public seats close by,
Inch down into their loosened flesh, each fold
Being sensible of the gravity
Which tugs
And longs to bring it down
And break its hold.

I walk between the kerb and bench
Conscious at length
Of sharing through each sense,
As if the light revealed us all
Sustained in delicate difference
Yet firmly growing from a single branch.

If that were all of it!
The branch that we grow on
Is not remembered easily in the dark,
Or the transparency when light is gone:
At most, a recollection
In the mind only—over a rainswept park
Held to by mere conviction
In cold and misery when the clock strikes one.

The lamp still shines.
The pale leaves shift a bit,
Now light, now shadowed, and their movement shared
A second later by the bough,
Even by the sap that runs through it:
A small full trembling through it now
As if each leaf were, so, better prepared
For falling sooner or later separate.

B12/4